THE U.S. SENATE

by Martha E. H. Rustad

PEBBLE
a capstone imprint

Pebble Explore is published by Pebble, an imprint of Capstone.
1710 Roe Crest Drive
North Mankato, Minnesota 56003
www.capstonepub.com

Library of Congress Cataloging-in-Publication Data is available on the Library of Congress website.
ISBN 978-1-9771-1397-9 (hardcover)
ISBN 978-1-9771-1821-9 (paperback)
ISBN 978-1-9771-1405-1 (ebook pdf)

Summary: Describes a senator's duties, how they are elected, where they work, and more.

Image Credits
Alamy: Dmitriy Shironosov, Cover; AP Images: J. Scott Applewhite, 19; Library of Congress Prints and Photographs, 26; NASA, 28; Newscom: CQ Roll Call/Bill Clark, 21, CQ Roll Call/Chris Maddaloni, 15, Jeff Malet Photography, 9, 23, Polaris/CNP/Leslie E. Kossoff, 17, Reuters/Joseph Menn, 5, Reuters/Joshua Roberts, 18, TNS/Joe Burbank, 11, ZUMA Press/Cecil Stoughton, 25; Shutterstock: Alexkava, 6 (middle), america365, 6 (left, right), lazyllama, 4; Wikimedia: Gage Skidmore from Peoria, AZ, United States of America, 13, Unites States Senate, 20

Design Elements
Shutterstock: ExpressVectors, In-Finity

Editorial Credits
Anna Butzer, editor; Cynthia Della-Rovere, designer;
Jo Miller, media researcher; Laura Manthe, production specialist

All internet sites appearing in back matter were available and accurate when this book was sent to press.

Printed and bound in China.
2489

Table of Contents

Words in **bold** are in the glossary.

What Is the Senate?

Everybody needs rules. You follow rules at home. There are rules at school too. People also follow rules called laws. The U.S. **government** makes our country's laws. The Senate is part of our government.

The Senate meets on Capitol Hill in Washington, D.C.

The U.S. government has three branches, or parts. A group called **Congress** makes our country's laws. It is part of the **legislative branch**. Congress has two parts. One part is the **House of Representatives**. The other part is the **Senate**. The Senate has 100 members.

Each branch of government has different rules to follow. Each has different jobs to do. All branches work together.

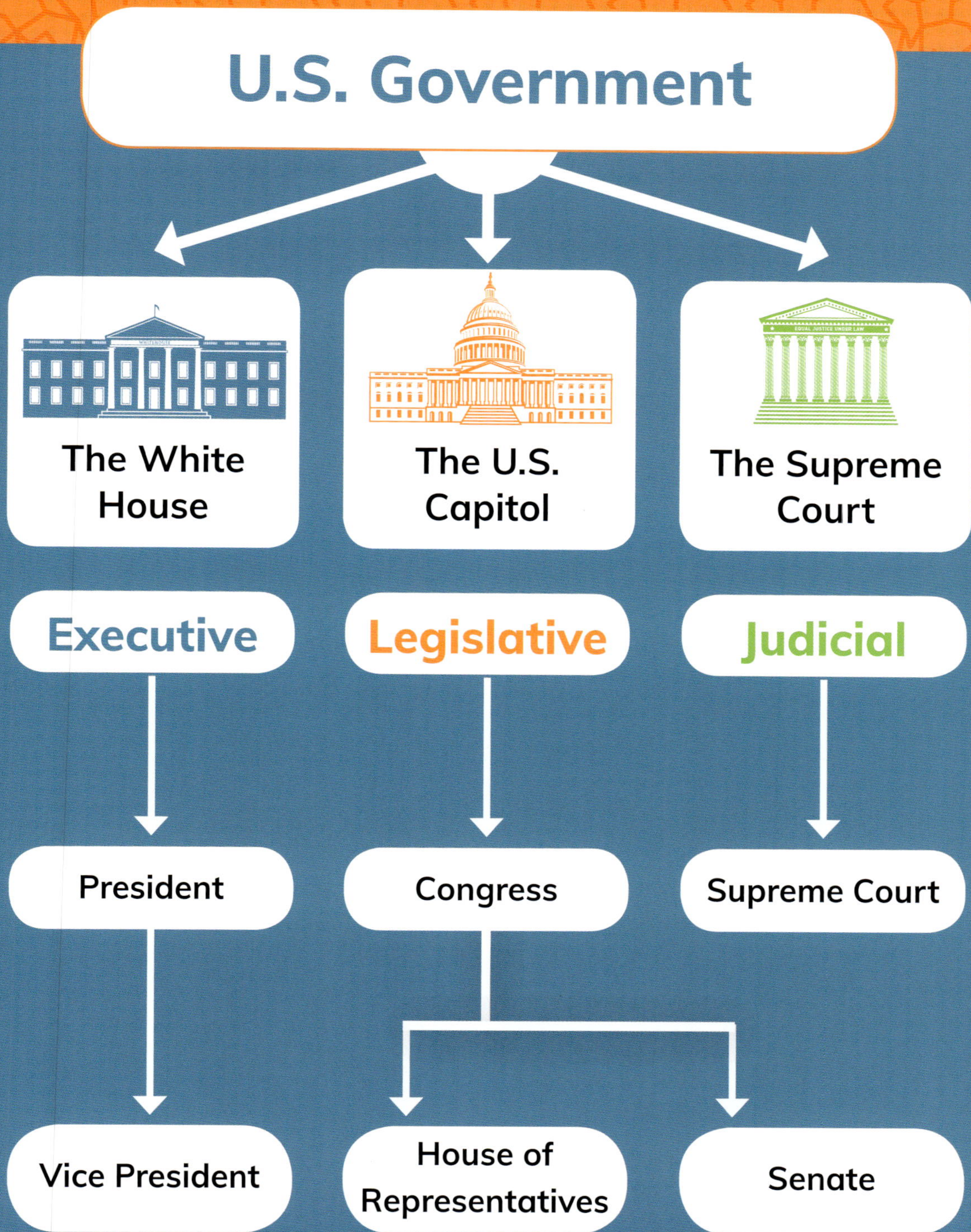
U.S. Government
The White House
The U.S. Capitol
The Supreme Court
EQUAL JUSTICE UNDER LAW
Executive
Legislative
Judicial
President
Congress
Supreme Court
Vice President
House of Representatives
Senate

Who Can Be a Senator?

Do you want to be a senator? There are rules about who can be one.

Senators must be at least 30 years old. They must be born in the United States. Or their parents must be born here. They must have lived in the country for at least nine years. Senators must live in the state they lead. A senator from Texas must live in Texas.

A senator is sworn into office.

Most senators start out in other jobs. Some were teachers. Some were doctors. Many were lawyers or writers. Some have been soldiers or actors. A few were astronauts!

Senators may seem very different. But all senators want to help others. They want to make their states better places to live.

Every senator works to make their state better.

How Are Senators Chosen?

How does someone get to be a senator? First people must become **candidates**. Then they travel all over their states. They talk with others. They listen to ideas. They tell people how they will help.

Citizens choose most leaders of government. On **Election Day** people in each state **vote**. They choose two senators in each state. Candidates with the most votes win.

A candidate shares ideas and plans for her state.

A senator's **term** lasts six years. Then the senator can run for office again. People vote to decide if that person can serve again. Sometimes they choose someone new.

Senators can stay in office as long as they keep getting elected. There are no limits on the number of terms a senator can serve. One senator served for more than 50 years!

Many senators serve more than one term.

What Does the Senate Do?

The Senate works closely with the House of Representatives. Together they write new laws for the country. The Senate also decides on the president's choices for other leaders.

A senator or representative writes a **bill**. That's a plan for a new law. They talk about the plan. They make changes. Then they vote. The vote decides if the bill should go to the president.

If the president signs the bill, it becomes law. Sometimes the president doesn't like the bill. Then the president does not sign it. Instead, it goes back to Congress for more changes.

The president signs a bill after it has passed through both parts of Congress.

Senators also meet in small groups. The groups are called **committees**. They talk about ideas for things such as schools and farms.

Senators are really busy! Other people help them. These workers help write speeches. They meet with people. They tell senators what they learned.

A worker follows a senator to meetings and takes notes.

Where Do Senators Work?

Senators work in the Capitol building in Washington, D.C. The Senate meets in a room called the Senate Chamber. Each senator sits at a desk in the chamber.

Senate Chamber in Washington, D.C.

A private subway takes senators to the Capitol.

Each senator also has an office in a nearby building. There they meet with people. They write letters and make phone calls. This building has more than offices. Senators can use its gym and pool. They also have their own subway! It takes them to the Capitol.

Senators don't always work in Washington, D.C. They also have offices in their home states. There they can listen to people in their states. Senators take the people's ideas back to Washington, D.C. Sometimes those ideas become new laws!

A senator talks about new ideas and listens to people from his home state.

Notable Senators

Since 1789 there have been nearly 2,000 U.S. senators. The shortest time a senator worked was one day. The longest time was 51 years!

SENATE SIBLINGS

Brothers have been senators at the same time! Theodore and Dwight Foster were both senators from 1800 to 1803. Edward and Robert Kennedy served together from 1965 to 1968.

Robert Kennedy (left) and Edward Kennedy (center)

FIRST WOMAN

In 1922 Rebecca Latimer Felton was the first female senator. She was from Georgia.

Rebecca Latimer Felton

LONGEST TIME ON THE JOB

Robert Byrd of West Virginia was senator from 1959 to 2010. He holds the record for the longest term. He served 51 years and 176 days.

SENATORS AND PRESIDENTS

Barack Obama was a senator before being president. John F. Kennedy and James Monroe were senators too. John Quincy Adams and Andrew Johnson were both senators after being president.

ASTRONAUT AND SENATOR

John Glenn went to space in 1962. He joined the Senate in 1974. In 1988 he became the only person to go to space while being a senator.

John Glenn

Fast Facts

Role: United States Senate

Job: Senators represent citizens in Washington, D.C. They talk about and write new laws for the country.

How Senators Are Chosen: Voters in their home states elect senators. Senators serve their states for six years.

Famous Senators: President Barack Obama was a senator for Illinois. Rebecca Latimer Felton of Georgia was the first woman to serve in the Senate. Hiram Revels of Mississippi was the first black senator.

Pay: The first senators earned $6 per day in 1789. Today senators earn $174,000 per year.

Glossary

bill (BIL)—a plan for a law

candidate (KAN-duh-dayt)—a person who wants a job in government

Capitol (KA-puh-tuhl)—a building where lawmakers meet

citizen (SI-tuh-zuhn)—a member of a country; a person becomes a citizen at birth or when they choose to become one as an adult.

committee (kuh-MI-tee)—a small group of senators or representatives formed to write and discuss bills

Congress (KAHNG-gruhs)—the government body of the United States that makes laws

election (i-LEK-shuhn)—the act of choosing people to work in government

government (GUHV-urn-muhnt)—the group of people who make laws, rules, and decisions for a country or state

House of Representatives (HOUSS UHV rep-ri-ZEN-tuh-tivs)—one of two houses in the U.S. Congress that makes laws

legislative branch (LEJ-iss-lay-tiv BRANCH)— one of the three parts of the U.S. government; this part makes rules and laws

Senate (SEN–it)— one of the two houses of Congress that makes laws

term (TERM)—a set amount of time for a job

vote (VOHT)—choice made by a person based on their own views

Read More

McAuliffe, Bill. *The U.S. Senate*. Mankato, MN: Creative Education, 2017.

Radomski, Kassandra. *So You Want to Be a U.S. Senator*. North Mankato, MN: Capstone, 2020.

Rose, Simon. *Senate*. New York: Smartbook Media, Inc., 2018.

Internet Sites

Architect of the Capitol: Panoramic Views
https://www.aoc.gov/multimedia-gallery/360-panoramic-views

Kids Clerk: How a Bill Becomes a Law
https://kids-clerk.house.gov/grade-school/lesson.html?intID=17

Welcome to the U.S. Capitol
http://www.visitthecapitol.gov

Index